The Christmas Challenge

Why the big party?

By Christina Gorham
Illustrations by Roxy T.

If you like this, you'll love:

The Lent Challenge

An opportunity to read about Jesus every day during Lent.

The Lent Challenge is formatted in a similar way to The Christmas Challenge while providing the bigger challenge of working through many stories and events of Jesus' life as you count down the days to Easter Sunday.

Coming soon:

The Easter Challenge

This is the sequel to The Christmas Challenge.

Designed for you to read in the same way as the Christmas Challenge, The Easter Challenge takes you on a journey through the events of Easter week as part of a twice weekly study during Lent.

Acknowledgements & Dedication

With many thanks to my beautiful children, who's births inspired the telling of so many stories. I would also like to thank the gifted women Linda E. Tipping and her daughter Roxy, who edited & illustrated this series, without you this book would be far less than it is.

May God bless you all.

Introduction

Advent lasts four weeks, culminating with the Jesus birthday party. Unfortunately, this fact is often lost amid the decorations, fun and games.

I challenge you to remember the reason for the season by joining me twice a week to re-live the events that made Christmas so important.

In this seven-week study (from the start of Advent to the end of Epiphany) you will get to explore the entire birth narrative, correcting some common myths and including bits many churches miss out.

What will you discover as we remember the birth of the Jewish Messiah, born to save all who will trust in him?

Bonus Story (Wednesday before Advent)

Zechariah's First Passover

Zechariah was so excited to be allowed to stay up and join in this year. Dad had said he could help with part of the Passover telling because he was finally old enough to join in. He bounced around the room, getting in the way as his mother set the table and explained to him what everything meant.

He suddenly spotted something that made him giggle. He'd been learning to count and could now make it all the way up to twenty. He'd just practiced his counting on the chairs around the table and discovered there were thirteen chairs, but he knew they were only expecting twelve people for Passover, Mum had said so.

"Mum." He asked, "Why are there thirteen chairs? There are only twelve of us. Did you count me twice?"

His mother laughed, "Hoping to get seconds Zechariah? There will be plenty of food. Don't you worry about your tummy." Then, more thoughtfully, she began to count carefully pointing at each chair as she went. "You are right. There is an extra place, but I will not take it away. It has been prepared for Elijah. We always set an extra place for him at Passover just in case he comes back and decides to visit us this year. It is important we are able to offer hospitality and he is a very important man. When he comes back, we will know the Messiah is nearly here."

"But didn't Dad say last Sabbath that Elijah died a long time ago?" Zechariah's dad was the village priest who often led the teaching in the local synagogue. He also taught in the school, ensuring all the local children could read, write and count accurately while teaching them the Torah, the word of God. One day this would be Zechariah's job too. This was why he asked so many questions, he knew he had to get it right.

His mum replied, "Elijah lived a long time ago, but he didn't die. God took him up to heaven in a chariot of fire. God promised Elijah would come back to prepare the way for the Messiah, so it's important we are ready for him. No one knows exactly when he will come, but I have a feeling you will get to meet him."

Now read

> 2 Kings 2:1-14
> Isaiah 40:3–5
> Malachi 4:5-6

My Notes

1st Sunday Of Advent

Birth Of John The Baptist Is Foretold

Zechariah and his wife Elizabeth had been married so long they should have been grandparents, but they weren't. This was because they had never been parents. They had never had any children.

One day Zechariah was working in the temple. (The temple was the main place of worship for the Jews. It looked a bit like a big church or cathedral). He was chosen for a very special job; this was the first and possibly last time he would get to go so close to the most holy place and offer God burnt incense and prayer just outside the curtain. He knew exactly what he had to do having been taught this as a child. He stepped forward with his special gift for God and did everything he was meant to do, including saying a special prayer for the Jews.

As he was turning to leave an angel appeared saying, "Do not be afraid!" Can you imagine how he must have felt to suddenly see an angel? The angel had a message for Zechariah. "You will be a father. Your wife Elizabeth will have a baby boy and you are to call him John. He will have the spirit of Elijah."

What a surprise that must have been! Not only to see a real angel but to hear that he and his wife were going to have a son after all these years of waiting. But not just any son, he would be a son of promise, blessed with the spirit of Elijah. This was more than they had dared to dream of, let alone pray for. Their son would herald the arrival of the Messiah.

Zechariah's reply was not so surprising; "Wow! You mean me? Really? I'm going to be a dad? That's just not possible!"

Angered by this response to such good news the angel told Zechariah off. "How dare you doubt my words by saying it's not possible? I am Gabriel. I stand in the presence of God! This will prove to you that God can do anything, even making you a father in your old age. You will not be able to talk until the child is born!"

And that's just what happened. From that moment until the birth of John, Zechariah was completely silent. If he wanted to tell someone something, he had to write it down.

Now read

Luke 1:5-25

My Notes

1ˢᵗ **Wednesday Of Advent**

A Letter Home

"Dear Dad

Thank you for your letter and the food you sent. Believe me, we all enjoyed sharing Mum's homemade treats. University in Babylon is brilliant and challenging. My teachers say that if I keep working hard, I could be his best student.

I've been learning about the history of Babylon and the different people who were brought here during the Babylonian empire. It's not so boring as it sounds.

Did you know that nearly six hundred years ago King Nebuchadnezzar brought the entire population of Judea over here? One of them became the King's most important adviser, Belteshazzar (Daniel to his people). He left us loads of information about the Jews, including copies of their holy scriptures that are still being read.

While reading these scriptures I've come across some confusing bits that appear to be talking about a king who will come to rule the world. Here are two extracts.

'I see him, but not now; I behold him, but not soon - a star will step forth from Jacob, a sceptre will arise from Israel, … A ruler will come out of Jacob'

'May his empire stretch from sea to sea, from The River to the ends of the earth. May desert-dwellers bow before him; may his enemies lick the dust.'

Obviously, with my name meaning 'star', I love the bit about a rising star but it's still confusing. Is it talking about an actual star or someone who is dressed so well they look like one? Is it talking about a God or a man? Daniel always prayed when he felt confused, and his God helped him. I think I'll try asking his God to explain these bits to me. I hope he gives me an answer before I grow as old as you.

Another bit that confuses me is how the Jews acted when they were slaves in Egypt. Pharaoh gave orders that the children had to be killed but the Jews rebelled. Why was the king so scared of babies? It's not like one of them wanted to steal his throne.

I'll write again soon. Give my love to everyone.

Your Son, Akhtar"

Now read

Numbers 24:17-19
Psalm 72:9,10
 Exodus 1:9-10, 15-22
Jeremiah 31:15

My Notes

2nd **Sunday Of Advent**

Birth Of Jesus Christ Is Foretold

About six months after Zechariah saw the angel, Mary was busy at home looking forward to her wedding day. She was engaged to a wonderful young man called Joseph. A carpenter and builder by trade, he was busy building the home they would live in. She knew the date for the wedding would not be set until their new house was ready for them to move in.

As she worked, singing about God and his promises,

the angel Gabriel suddenly appeared to her. "Do not be afraid Mary. I have a fantastic message for you. You are the most blessed woman of all time, because God has chosen you to be the mother of his son, the Messiah. You must call the boy Jesus."

Mary had just one question; "How is this possible? I've never slept with, or even kissed a man before." She knew it was not possible for a woman to have a baby without the help of a man and that if she was found to have a child before getting married, her life and the baby's life would be in danger because people would think she had broken the law. She also knew that with God all things are possible.

Gabriel explained that it would be a miracle performed by God himself, so that there could be no doubt that the son born to Mary would also be the Son of God.

"Ok." Mary's simple reply with faith that if God says it will happen, then it will happen, pleased and stunned the angel causing him to look in wonder and amazement at this unique woman. He had one final bit of news for Mary: "Your cousin Elizabeth, the one you all thought would never have children, is pregnant. She has been expecting a miracle son for the last six months."

Having delivered the message, the angel left Mary to think about what had happened, knowing that if God chose to make her the mother of his son, he would also ensure they survived in a land where women were stoned to death for having children without first having a husband.

Mary made a very important decision. She began to pack.

Now read

Luke 1:26-38

My Notes

2nd Wednesday Of Advent

Caiaphas' First Day At School

Caiaphas skipped eagerly down the road. "Hurry up Annas! We don't want to be late."

His face breaking into a broad grin, Annas ran up behind his friend, scooped him up onto his shoulders and ran, laughing down the road. There may have been six years between them but that didn't stand between their friendship.

They slowed as they reached the corner afraid

of bumping into the Rabbi. They both knew that Annas, approaching his twelfth birthday and manhood, would suffer for such behaviour if they were caught.

"What do you think we'll be learning about today?" Caiaphas asked his companion as they walked side by side around the corner. "Noah and the flood? Isaac's birthday? King David and the giant?"

Laughing merrily at his companion's eager questions, Annas replied, "You'll probably start with the alphabet. There's no point in learning to write the scriptures before you can read them. Rabbi usually lets the youngest class choose a story or two in the afternoon so you may get your choice then, but you mustn't be too disappointed if he selects something different."

"What about you? What will you be learning in your class?"

"Last week I was studying the prophet Micah. I'll probably have a test today to see if I've correctly memorised the entire book. I like it when we start digging into the prophet's words, trying to understand the prophecies."

"Oooh! Can you recite some for me? I know I won't get to study Micah for a long time."

"Ok. How about this bit?

    "But you, Bethlehem near Ephrata, so small among the clans of Judah, out of you will come forth to me the future ruler of Israel, whose origins are far in the past, back in ancient times."

"What does it mean?" Caiaphas continued to quiz Annas all the way there and Annas did his best to answer his young pupil. This was good practice if he wanted to become high priest one day.

Now read

Micah, 5:2

Genesis 6-9:17 (yes, it's long but you can skip bits if you're short on time)

Genesis 18:1-15 & 21:1-7

1 Samuel 17

My Notes

3rd Sunday Of Advent

John Is Born

It had been a long walk with the group of travellers from her home in Nazareth to cousin Elizabeth in the hills near Jerusalem, but after nearly a week Elizabeth's village was finally in view. Mary rested to wash by the village well before looking for her cousin's home.

As Mary entered the house she called out "Hallo! Elizabe…?" She would have said more but Elizabeth interrupted her as she burst into the room full of joy and praise to God. "Glory to God! What a wonderful thing to be visited by the mother of our LORD!" Elizabeth didn't know that Mary's son would be called Jesus, but she did know he was the Son of God. Then she explained that the moment Mary had spoken, the baby inside her had jumped so high in excitement at meeting the baby inside Mary, that she simply had to shout out the words God gave her to shout.

Over the coming days the two women spent a lot of time talking about their babies, what the scriptures said about them, as well as their hopes and dreams for the two boys. They were preparing for the birth of John and Jesus together.

Finally, the time came for John to be born and Mary was there to help her cousin. Then came the friends and family, all the neighbours, in fact everyone who lived close enough to visit came to the home of Zechariah and Elizabeth to celebrate with them over the new baby boy and to formally give him his name.

"Let's call him Zechariah after his father" came the unanimous decision of the guests. Even after Elizabeth said "No! His name is John." They didn't want to listen to her, a woman, so it was up to Zechariah to convince all the visitors that his wife was speaking the truth. As he could not speak Zechariah had only one way to tell everyone the name of his son. He asked for something to write with and wrote, "His name is John." Immediately he was able to speak, and he began praising God for the wonderful miracle of his son.

The people accepted that the child was called John and went away wondering what sort of man he would grow up to be.

Now read

Luke 1:39-80 (57-66)

My Notes

3rd Wednesday Of Advent

Building A Home

"I bring food for the worker!" Simon shouted as he approached the almost completed house. "Joseph! Where are you?"

Joseph's head appeared over the top of the house. He'd been working on the roof struts. "Good to see you, Simon. What's that about food and what's that smell?"

"You missed dinner again, so Mum sent me over with some bread and fish soup. Come on down and eat." As he spoke Joseph slid down a ladder and strode over to his younger brother, realizing he was rather hungry. "I'm under orders to make certain you "eat it all like a good boy." His impression of their mum making both men laugh and nearly spilling the soup.

Joseph had come to work on this building site as soon as his shift on the building site he was paid to work at had finished. He was determined to finish building his own home as soon as possible; only then could he marry Mary.

"You're crazy building a house in Nazareth." The statement took Joseph by surprise. He raised an enquiring eyebrow, mid-mouthful. "You do realize you only rented the land? In a few years it'll go back to its original owner and your family will be kicked out."

Swallowing his bread, Joseph replied, "It's over thirty years until the next Jubilee year. I've got plenty of time to build up the business and save up enough money to rent the land with the house again, or move to a better place if I have too many children for this small place." Laughing at his own joke, he slapped his brother on the back.

Simon didn't join in the merriment. "But aren't you worried something could happen? All this hard work, time and money spent on materials could be lost in an instant."

"You worry too much Brother. Our family still have

the house and land in Bethlehem. Nothing bad is going to happen. You'll see. It's not like the virgin is about to give birth to the promised Messiah?"

Now read

> Isaiah 7:14
> Leviticus 25:10-13

My Notes

4th Sunday Of Advent

Journey To Bethlehem

"I've been so busy since returning from Elizabeth's. It all began when I arrived back, full of news of John, but Joseph ran away from me crying. It shouldn't have been a surprise; I hadn't told Joseph about the angel's visit. Joseph could see I was pregnant and thought I had broken God's laws about marriage and that he would no longer be able to marry me. The feeling of betrayal must have been so hard because we both knew he was not the father. He had begun to plan how to break the engagement in a way that would not endanger my life for, despite it all, he still loved me. Thankfully, God sent an angel to Joseph in a dream who explained everything. Joseph married me as soon as possible because that's what the angel in his dream had told him to do, but does he trust me?"

"Mary!" Joseph's shout interrupted her thoughts as he ran into the house. "Caesar wants to count us all. We have been ordered to return to our hometowns and register for tax. If we leave now, we should make it before you give birth. What better place for the Son of God to be born than in Bethlehem, the town of David? We can even give him a proper welcome at the temple." Having delivered his message Joseph ran out again to buy supplies for the long walk. He knew it normally took nearly a week and probably more now with Mary so close to giving birth, but they didn't have a choice. They had to go.

Early the next day, the young couple left Nazareth on the long walk to Bethlehem. They didn't have a donkey; they were too poor for that. Joseph had repaired his old hand cart for the journey. It was loaded with all the things they would need, from food and a small tent to a change of clothing and his tool kit.

Joseph intended to work in Bethlehem while the baby was small. Hopefully they would be more welcome there than in Nazareth, and he would be able to build up the business he'd ruined by marrying Mary despite the baby she carried. He expected, one day to return to the home he'd spent so much time preparing for them.

As they set out there was just one thing niggling at them, would they make it in time? The unspoken question kept going around both of their minds.

Now read

> Matthew 1:18-25
> Luke 2:1-5

My Notes

Christmas Day

Jesus Is Born

It had been a long journey. Much longer than they had expected. It was now late in the day, and they had finally made it up the hill to Bethlehem. Mary rested while Joseph knocked at the doors of relatives. Always the answer was the same, "No Room." Mary was not welcome because of her unborn child.

This was the last house in the village. It belonged to the innkeeper. They couldn't really afford to pay for a room, but they didn't have a choice. Joseph braced himself and knocked again. The innkeeper's wife opened the door. "Sorry. It's the census you see. Every room is full." But she saw Mary resting there, silently, knowing the time for her to give birth was very close. The woman felt compassion for the couple stood at her door. "There's the stable just out of town. It's not where I'd want to have my child, but I can't think of anywhere else with a roof and walls that might have space for you."

So that's how they came to be making camp in a stable full of sheep when, "Joseph! Find help! It's time!" He ran into the night to find anyone who would be willing to help bring the Son of God into the world. Meanwhile, Mary did everything she had learnt when she helped her cousin Elizabeth give birth to John. She laboured late into the night while Joseph prayed - he could do nothing more - until they heard the sound they had both waited so long to hear. Baby Jesus cried. Joseph cried waiting for Mary to invite him back in. Mary cried with joy and relief calling to her husband to come and greet his new son, Jesus.

Those first quiet moments, when only they knew of this new life were so precious. As Mary hugged Jesus and Joseph kissed them both, they knew that any doubts they still had when they arrived in Bethlehem had gone - completely evaporating as they gazed into the eyes so full of love and let their hearts melt towards the saviour of the world.

They knew it would not be easy to raise such a child, but they knew with God's help he would thrive.

Now read

Luke 2:6-7

My Notes

Sunday After Christmas

The Shepherds Visit

It was late, no one knows quite how late, but I expect that if shepherds had socks, they would have finished washing and drying them long before! All the sheep were settled safely sleeping the night away as the shepherds kept watch for dangers of the night. It was not unheard of for a wild animal to steal lambs when it was too dark for the shepherd to see them. They were casually talking about the day, quietly helping each other stay alert when…

Suddenly there was a brilliant, bright angel standing in front of the group of shepherds.

They were terrified. Even after the angel had joyfully told them to not be afraid and that he had the best news for them. The shepherds may have been paralysed by fear, but they were listening very hard and remembering every word.

"God's son has been born to save the entire world! He's wrapped simply in strips of cloth and sleeping in the sheep water trough. Quickly go and find him!"

Then the angel was joined by thousands upon thousands of others all singing praise to God for the wonder he had just done. There could be no doubt. This was no dream; it was real, and they had to act fast. So, as soon as the shepherds had regained their night vision, they left their sheep unguarded and raced to Bethlehem to search for and find the baby Messiah and to worship the one born to bring salvation to the world.

When they found the baby, what a commotion they made. First, they had to wake up Mary and Joseph to tell them what the angels had said. Then they all wanted to see this baby and bless it as best they knew how. But after all this they went out and woke up everyone in Bethlehem, in the early morning light, to tell them about the new baby in the manger and what the angels had said to them out in the fields.

The shepherds didn't return to their sheep until everyone had heard the good news about this special baby boy.

Now read

Luke 2:8-20

My Notes

Wednesday Before Epiphany

The Prophets Simeon And Anna

Jesus was now forty days old and doing everything you would expect from a new-born baby (sleep, eat, poo and cry if he wanted anything). You could tell how very proud his parents were just by looking at them, how they laughed and played with their first child. It didn't matter that Joseph was not the real father, he loved Jesus as if he were.

It was time to take Jesus to the temple and thank God for the gift of a new baby by giving a sacrifice and presenting the child to the Lord, dedicated to doing the will of God all the days of his life, as the law required.

While Mary and Joseph were in the temple a man called Simeon approached them. He was very old, and he was a prophet. The Holy Spirit had told him he would not die before he has seen the Messiah, the one born to save everyone. Today the Holy Spirit had told him to go to the temple.

As soon as he saw the small family, he knew this was the promised child. He eagerly went to hold and bless the infant. He thanked God for keeping his promises to himself and to the nation of Israel by sending the Saviour. Simeon blessed Jesus and spoke words of prophecy over Mary, "This child is destined to cause the falling and rising of many in Israel, and to be a sign that will be spoken against, so that the thoughts of many hearts will be revealed, and a sword will pierce your own soul too."

Before Mary could ask what those words meant, a very old woman came up, the widowed prophetess Anna, who lived in the temple. She also thanked God for this child, but she didn't prophesy over the family as Simeon had, she told everyone who would listen about this miracle child born to be the promised Messiah.

We don't know how many people heard about baby Jesus that day or how many listened and remembered what they were told. We do know that Mary remembered every word and treasured them up in her heart thinking about them often over the coming weeks, months and years.

Now read

Luke 2:22-38

My Notes

Epiphany Sunday

The Wise Men

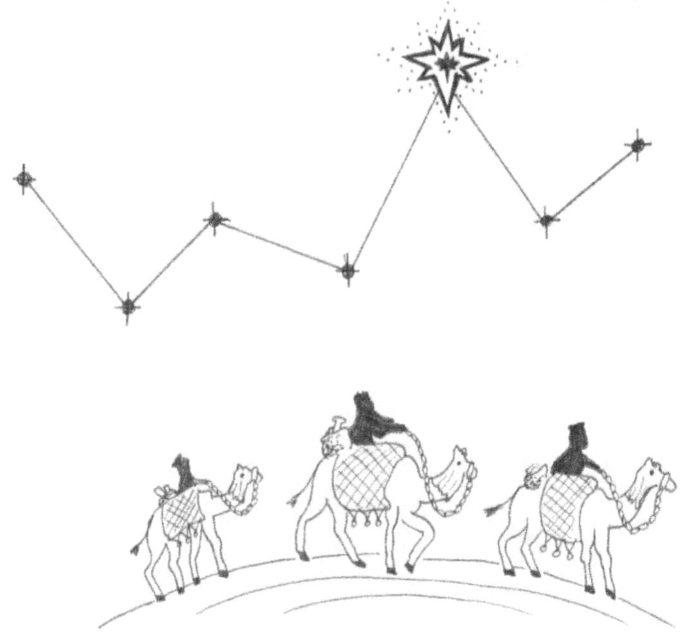

"Look! Come quickly! There's a new star!" The other men left their work and came to see what had made the night watcher so excited. They were all highly trained in many different subjects. Some were brilliant at maths others were astounding at languages (both their native one and foreign languages). Many were skilled scientists and historians, but the night watcher was especially good at watching the night sky and using it to set the calendar, navigate, and tell the future.

The men crowded round eager to see what had been found and to test it for truth. Yes, a new star, not on any of their charts or records. What could it mean? They searched the library, reading the books on astrology, history, other cultures and many more besides. Eventually, the group of men came back together and shared what they had learnt. This star meant a new King of the Jews had been born. He was a very special child. The books were not clear if he would be a king or a god, so the most important men decided to go to Jerusalem, find the child and give him a test.

Soon all was ready. The group of men left with their gifts on the long journey to Jerusalem. It would take them many months to cross the desert from Babylon.

When they arrived, they went straight to the palace in Jerusalem and asked to see the new baby king. When King Herod heard this, he was very upset because there was no baby or young child in the palace, and he could not risk someone else growing up to take his throne. He called for the wisest men in the city to find out what they knew. The teachers told him the ancient prophets said that the Messiah would be born in Bethlehem. So, Herod sent the foreigners to Bethlehem to search for the "new king" and report back to him.

The Wise Men searched and found the young child, Jesus in a house in Bethlehem. After explaining why they had travelled so far, they presented Jesus with three gifts to test what sort of king he would be. Jesus accepted the gold for a king, frankincense for a god, and myrrh for one who would die young (this spice was important for burial but so expensive it was often reserved for the richest and most important people). This caused the men to wonder even more, "What sort of king will he be?"

Now read

Matthew 2:1-12
Micah, 5:2

My Notes

Wednesday After Epiphany

A Close Escape

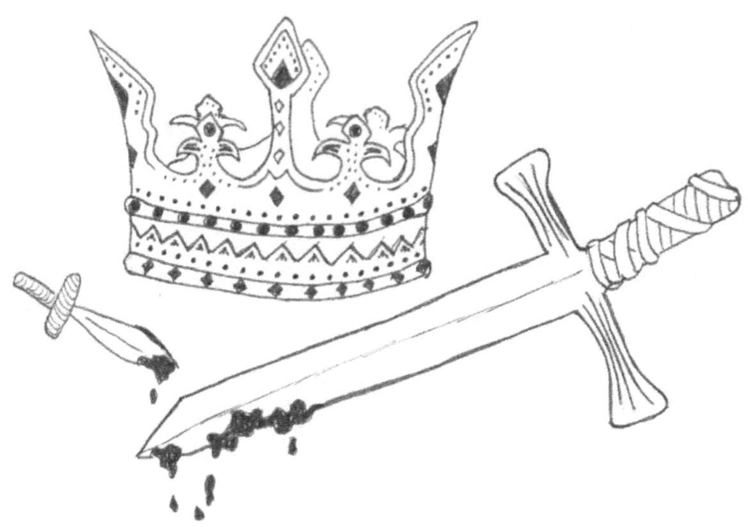

That night, while The Wise Men slept in Bethlehem, expecting to return to Jerusalem to keep their promise to Herod, they had a dream. An angel appeared to them and told them, "Do not go back to Herod or tell him where to find this child, because he wants to kill Jesus. Go home a different way." When they woke up, they all agreed this was a message from God that must be obeyed, even though it meant breaking a promise. They were careful to leave Bethlehem in secret and returned to their home across the eastern desert without going near Jerusalem.

Soon after, Joseph too had a dream of an angel. It

said "Quickly! Take Mary and Jesus and run to Egypt. Herod wants to kill the child." Joseph was so upset by the dream that he woke up immediately and shook Mary awake too. He told her the dream and they packed as quickly as they could. They would prepare properly for the long journey to Egypt in a different place, for now it was too dangerous, they had to escape before Herod's men arrived. The last thing they did before hurrying into the night was to pick Jesus up from his bed, being careful not to wake him, and to leave money on the table to pay for their stay.

Quietly the small family crept into the night. Being careful to not be seen by anyone, they moved from one shadow to the next. Finding the road south they started to walk as best they could in the dark night. Not until morning did they stop to rest, taking care to find a hidden place because they were still too close to Bethlehem and Jerusalem.

After a few days it was safe for them to travel by day in the normal way so that when they came to a small town, they could find a room and prepare for the long journey to Egypt. Hopefully they would find a trading caravan they could join. It would be much safer to travel with them, and that way they would not need to hire a guide across the southern desert. While they were preparing, news reached them of the terrible things Herod had done when he found out the wise men had broken their promise.

Now read

> Matthew 2:13-18
> Hosea 11:1
> Jeremiah 31:15

My Notes

One Last Story

Boy At The Temple

The years passed and Jesus grew into a clever youth who loved to learn about God, his father. By this time his family had moved back to Nazareth and he had younger brothers and sisters.

When he was twelve his family prepared, as usual, to walk to Jerusalem for the feast of Passover. All his uncles were going too with their families meaning many of his friends were also going. They were travelling as one huge group because this was safer than travelling alone. This year was more special than usual because Jesus was coming of age; there would be a big celebration when he recited the large section of scripture, and he would soon need to choose the trade he would learn before setting up on his own as an adult.

When they finally got to Jerusalem the group had to split up, finding places to stay where they could in the crowded city. Some found rooms, many made camp on the hills nearby, but everyone wanted to party as they remembered how good God is and was hundreds of years before at the first Passover.

When the feast ended everyone packed up, gathering into one huge group for travelling back to Nazareth. No one noticed that Jesus was not in the bustling crowd. They had walked a long way when Mary and Joseph started to gather their children for the evening meal and to make camp for the night. That was when Mary found out Jesus wasn't there.

Fearing the worst, Mary and Joseph left their other children with a relative and hurried through the night back to Jerusalem. They spent three days searching the city, asking everyone they could if they had seen their eldest son.

Finally, they went to the Temple exhausted. They searched until they heard him. Jesus was sitting with the teachers, asking and answering questions with such wisdom that the teachers were very impressed. Mary didn't realise this; in her relief at finding him, she just ran up and told Jesus off for not returning with the rest of the group. Jesus was sorry for causing so much upset, but he knew what he was going to do next. He was going to learn to be a carpenter and builder, like his father, and a wandering rabbi, a teacher. All rabbis had a trade they could use to earn money, but they spent their free time studying God's word and teaching others.

Now read

Luke 2:41-52

My Notes

If you liked the Christmas challenge, you'll love the **Easter Challenge**.

Spend time as a family discovering the events of Easter, before, during and after the cross, because death is not the end.

If this was too easy a challenge for you,
have you tried **The Lent Challenge**?

I challenge you to read about Jesus
every day during Lent this year.
Will you make it to the end without skipping a day?

About The Author

Christina was 'born and bred' within the church community. She freely gave her life to the Lord as a child and has spent considerable time and effort since then getting to know her incredible God.

She may not be a qualified vicar, but she knows her Bible and has a unique ability to make it make sense, even for the youngest readers, bringing to life the centuries old truths for a new generation.

Happy Birthday to you
Happy Birthday to you
Happy Birthday dear Jesus
Happy Birthday to you

Let's rediscover Christmas truths as we enjoy family time. Sit together and read the events surrounding Jesus' birthday, retold for you in twice weekly short stories for all the family.

Look up the bible references, talk about these events, make notes, and colour in the unique illustrations that accompany every story. There's something for every family member to engage with.

What will you discover about Jesus this Christmas?